PAPER ROCKETS

Duy & Tramy Nguyen

STERLING INNOVATION
An imprint of Sterling Publishing Co., Inc.

New York / London
www.sterlingpublishing.com

STERLING, the Sterling logo, STERLING INNOVATION, and the
Sterling Innovation logo are registered trademarks of
Sterling Publishing Co., Inc.

2 4 6 8 10 9 7 5 3 1

Published by Sterling Publishing Co., Inc.
387 Park Avenue South, New York, NY 10016
© 2009 by Duy & Tramy Nguyen
Distributed in Canada by Sterling Publishing
c/o Canadian Manda Group, 165 Dufferin Street
Toronto, Ontario, Canada M6K 3H6
Distributed in the United Kingdom by GMC Distribution Services
Castle Place, 166 High Street, Lewes, East Sussex, England BN7 1XU
Distributed in Australia by Capricorn Link (Australia) Pty. Ltd.
P.O. Box 704, Windsor, NSW 2756, Australia

Printed in China

Sterling ISBN 978-1-4027-6111-9

For information about custom editions, special sales,
premium and corporate purchases, please contact
Sterling Special Sales Department at 800-805-5489
or specialsales@sterlingpublishing.com.

Contents

Basic Instructions

Paper

The best paper to use for origami will be very thin, keep a crease well, and fold flat. It can be plain white paper, solid-color paper, or wrapping paper with a design only on one side. Regular computer paper may be too heavy to allow the many tight folds needed for some figures. Be aware, too, that some kinds of paper may stretch slightly, either in length or in width, and this may cause a problem in paper folding. Packets of paper especially for use in origami are available from craft and hobby shops.

Unless otherwise indicated, the paper used in creating these forms is square, 15 by 15 centimeters or approximately 6 by 6 inches. A few origami forms require a more rectangular (legal) size or a longer piece of paper. For those who are learning and have a problem getting their fingers to work tight folds, larger sizes of paper can be used. Actually, any size paper squares can be used—slightly larger figures are easier to make than overly small ones. The two sizes of paper provided within this gift set are 6 by 6 inches and 3 3/4 by 9 3/4 inches, easy to work with for origami novices. The longer paper works well for the projects with rectangular starts. For some projects, an alternate size is suggested.

Glue

Use an easy-flowing but not loose paper glue. Use it sparingly; you don't want to soak the paper. A toothpick makes a good applicator. Allow the glued form time to dry. Avoid using stick glue, as the application pressure needed (especially if the stick has become dry) can damage your figure.

Technique

Fold with care. Position the paper precisely, especially at corners, and see that edges line up before creasing a fold. Once you are sure of the fold, use a fingernail to make a clean, flat crease. Don't get discouraged with your first efforts. In time, what your mind can create, your fingers can fashion.

Symbols & Lines

Valley fold   Mountain fold   Cut line

Turn over or
rotate

Fold then unfold

Pleat fold
(repeated folding)

Crease line

Basic Folds
Valley Fold

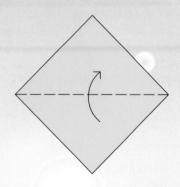 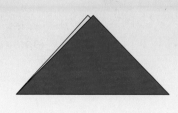

1. Fold form toward you (forward),
   making a "valley."

2. This fold forward is a valley fold.

Mountain Fold

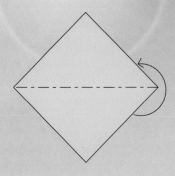 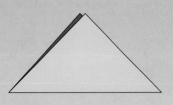

1. Fold form away from you (backward), making a "mountain."

2. This fold backward is a mountain fold.

Kite Fold

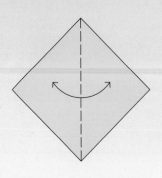 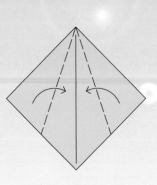 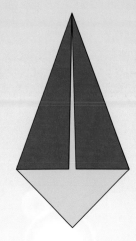

1. Fold and unfold a square diagonally, making a center crease.

2. Fold both sides in to the center crease.

3. This is a kite fold.

Inside Reverse Fold

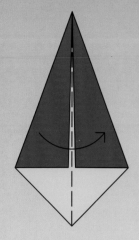

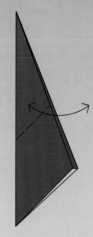

1. Starting here with a kite, valley fold kite closed.

2. Valley fold as marked to crease, then unfold.

3. Mountain fold to crease, then unfold.

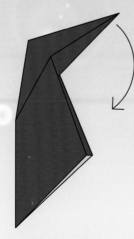

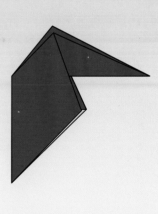

4. Pull tip in direction of arrow.

5. Appearance before completion.

6. This is an inside reverse fold.

Outside Reverse Fold

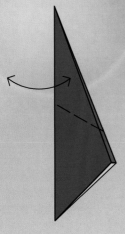

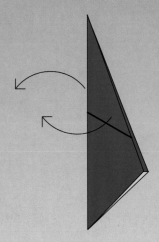

1. Using a closed kite, valley fold and unfold.

2. Fold inside out, as shown by arrows.

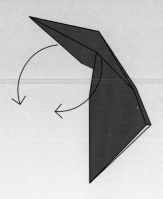

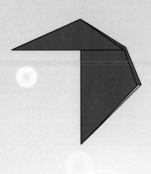

3. Appearance before completion.

4. This is an outside reverse fold.

Pleat Fold

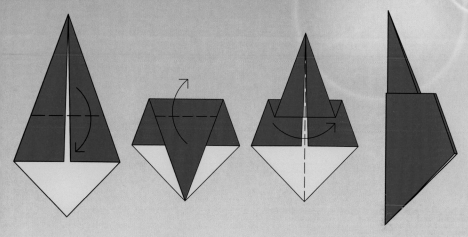

1. Using the kite, valley fold.

2. Valley fold back again for pleat.

3. This is a pleat fold. Valley fold in half.

4. This is a pleat fold form.

Pleat Fold Reverse

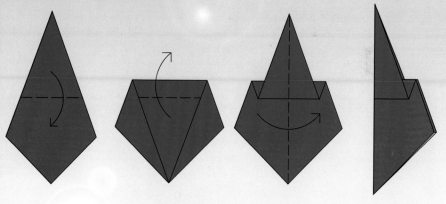

1. Using the kite form backward, valley fold.

2. Valley fold back again for pleat.

3. Valley fold form in half.

4. This is a pleat fold reverse form.

...ash Fold I

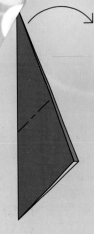
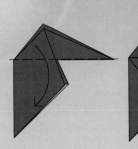
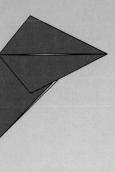

1. Using a closed kite form, inside reverse fold.

2. Valley fold front layer.

3. This is a squash fold I.

Squash Fold II

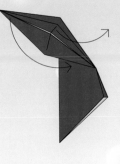

1. Using a closed kite form, valley fold.

2. Open in direction of the arrow.

3. Appearance before completion.

4. This is a squash fold II.

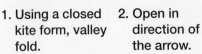

Inside Crimp Fold

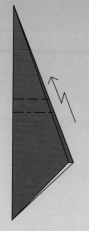 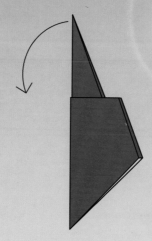 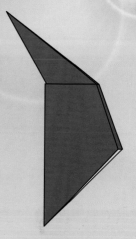

1. Using a closed kite form, pleat fold.

2. Pull tip in direction of arrow.

3. This is an inside crimp fold.

Outside Crimp Fold

1. Using a closed kite form, pleat fold and unfold.

2. Fold mountain and valley as shown, both sides.

3. This is an outside crimp fold.

ounding Rocket

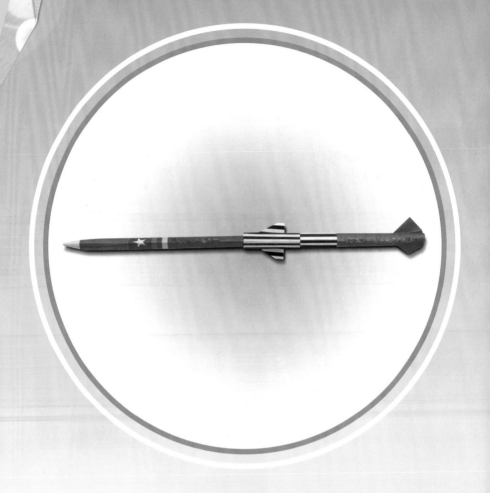

This two-staged sounding rocket is based on the United States Terrier-Improved Orion and is spin-stabilized. It is 41.9 feet (12.8 m) long, has a diameter of 1.5 feet (.46 m), and weighs an astounding 2,800 pounds (1,300 kg)! Sounding rockets are used to carry scientific instruments into space, without going into a full orbit, to perform experiments and take scientific readings.

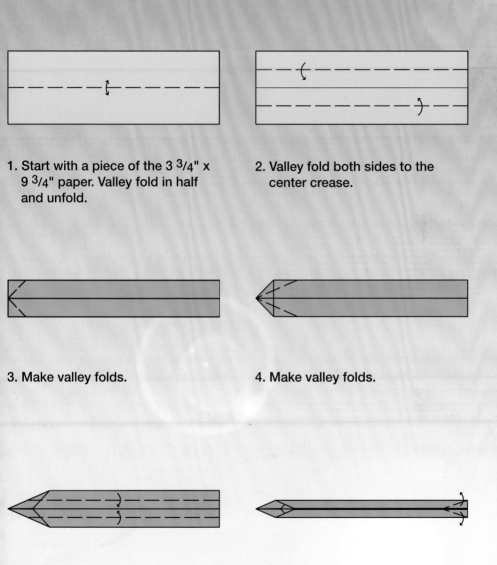

1. Start with a piece of the 3 3/4" x 9 3/4" paper. Valley fold in half and unfold.

2. Valley fold both sides to the center crease.

3. Make valley folds.

4. Make valley folds.

5. Make valley folds.

6. Make valley folds.

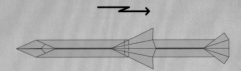

7. Make cuts to the top layers and then valley fold the cut parts.

8. Pleat fold.

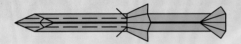

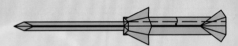

9. Make squash folds.

10. Valley fold.

11. Make valley folds.

12. Valley fold.

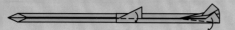

13. Make valley folds.

14. Make cuts as shown.

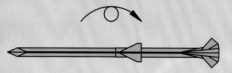

15. Turn over.

16. Add colors and patterns as desired.

17. Completed Sounding Rocket.

To Launch Rocket with Launcher:

Hold the launcher with the rubberband knot toward the front, underneath a dowel. Hold rocket over dowel and wrap the back of the rubberband over the back of the rocket, holding on to both the rocket and the rubberband. Pull rubberband back and release to launch rocket.

This surface-to-air naval missile is based on the British Seawolf Missile. Developed in the Cold War Era, this high-speed, close-range missile protects against anti-ship missiles. With a maximum speed of Mach 2, this missile has a range of 4 miles to 6.2 miles (6.5 km to 10 km), depending on the direction of the launch. It is a little over 6 feet tall (1.9 m), almost a foot (.3 m) in diameter, and weighs around 180 pounds (82 kg).

Part 1

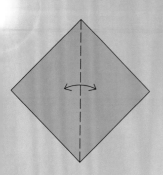

1. Valley fold and unfold.

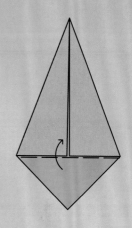

2. Kite fold.

3. Valley fold.

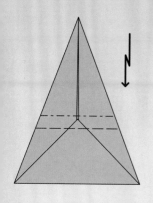

4. Pleat fold.

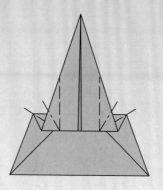

5. Make squash folds.

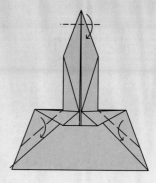

6. Make valley folds.

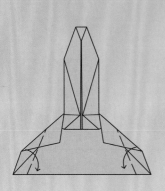

7. Make valley folds.

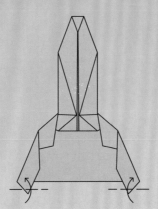

8. Make valley folds.

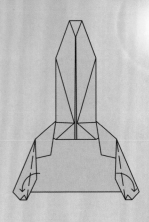

9. Make valley folds.

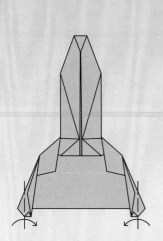

10. Make valley folds.

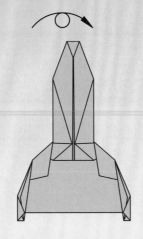

11. Rotate.

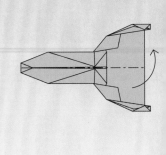

12. Mountain fold in half.

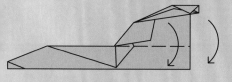

13. Valley fold both sides.

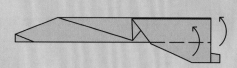

14. Valley fold both sides.

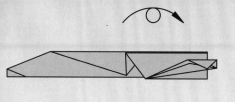

15. Rotate.

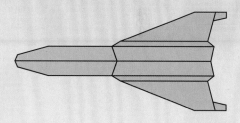

16. Completed part 1.

Part 2

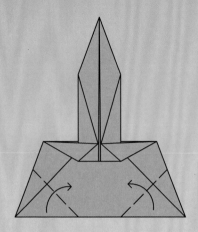

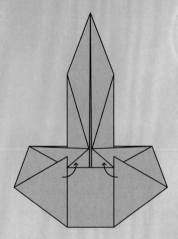

1. Complete steps 1 to 5 of Surface-to-Air Naval Anti-Missile Part 1. Make valley folds.

2. Hide tips behind previous layer.

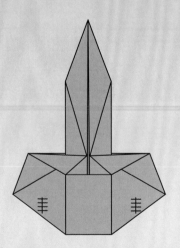

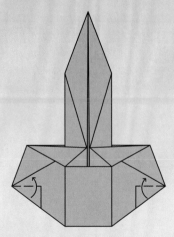

3. Make cuts as shown.

4. Make valley folds.

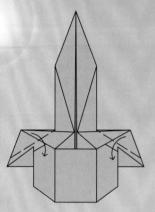

5. Make valley folds.

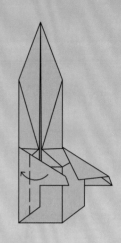

6. Valley fold.

7. Valley fold.

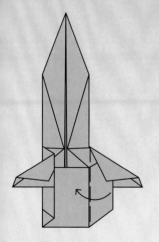

8. Valley fold.

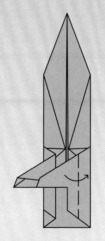

9. Valley fold.

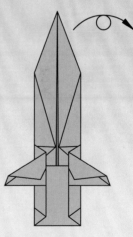

10. Turn over.

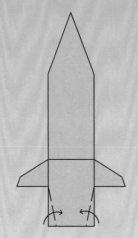

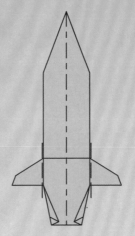

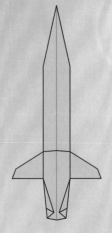

11. Make valley folds.

12. Mountain fold the center to crease slightly and valley fold the wings to be even.

13. Completed part 2.

TO ATTACH

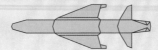

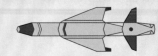

1. Insert part 2 into part 1 as shown and apply glue to hold.

2. Add colors and patterns as desired.

3. Completed Surface-to-Air Naval Anti-Missile.

Air-to-Surface Cruise Missile

This air-to-surface cruise missile is based on Israel's supposed Popeye Turbo cruise missile. While the official maximum range is between 124 to 217 miles (200 to 350 km), this cruise missile reportedly was successfully tested at a range of 932 miles (1,500 km).

Part 1

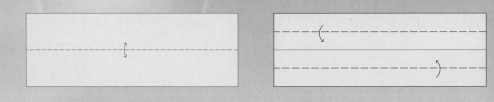

1. Start with a piece of the 3 3/4" x 9 3/4" paper. Valley fold in half and unfold.

2. Valley fold both sides to the center crease.

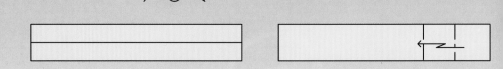

3. Turn over.

4. Pleat fold.

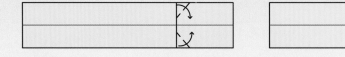

5. Make inside reverse folds.

6. Valley fold.

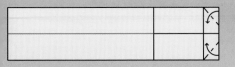

7. Make inside reverse folds.

8. Make valley folds.

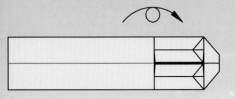

9. Turn over.

10. Make valley folds.

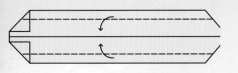

11. Make valley folds.

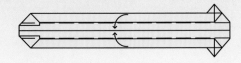

12. Make valley folds.

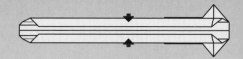

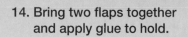

13. Unfold the last two steps.

14. Bring two flaps together and apply glue to hold.

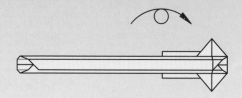

15. Turn over.

16. Bring two flaps together and apply glue to hold.

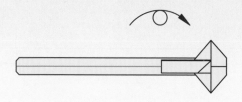

17. Turn over.

18. Completed part 1.

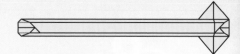

Part 2

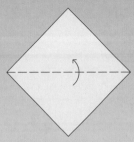

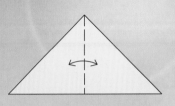

1. Start with a 3" by 3" paper. Valley fold.

2. Valley fold and unfold.

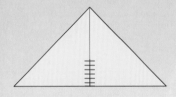

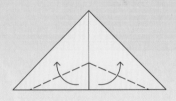

3. Make cut as shown.

4. Make valley folds.

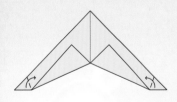

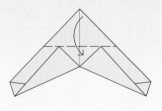

5. Make valley folds and hide tips behind the top layer.

6. Valley fold.

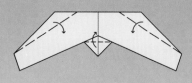

7. Turn over.

8. Make valley folds.

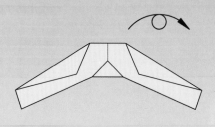

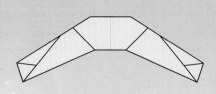

9. Turn over.

10. Completed part 2.

TO ATTACH

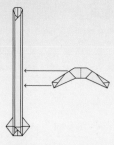

1. Place part 2 under part 1 as shown and apply glue to hold.

2. Completed Air-to-Surface Cruise Missile.

Air-to-Surface Guided Missile

This radio-guided short-range missile is based on the United States Navy's 1950s Bullpup missile. The maximum speed is approximately Mach 1.8, and the maximum range for the missile is 10 miles (16 km). It weighs around 1,785 pounds (810 kg), and has a height of approximately 13.6 feet (4.14 m), a diameter of 18 inches (.46 m), and a wingspan of 4 feet (1.22 m).

Part 1

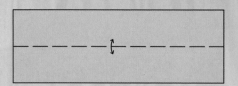

1. Start with a piece of the 3 3/4" x 9 3/4" paper. Valley fold in half and unfold.

2. Valley fold both sides to the center crease.

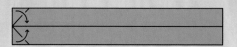

3. Make valley folds.

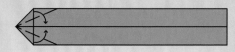

4. Make valley folds.

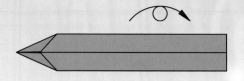

5. Turn over.

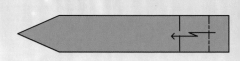

6. Pleat fold.

7. Make inside reverse folds.

8. Make cut and then valley fold.

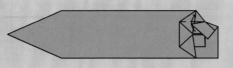

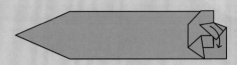

9. Valley fold bottom layer and hide behind top layer.

10. Hide flap behind layer.

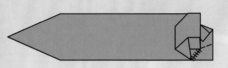

11. Make cut and then valley fold.

12. Valley fold bottom layer and hide behind bottom layer.

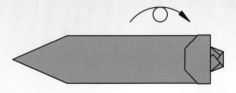

13. Hide flap behind layer.

14. Turn over.

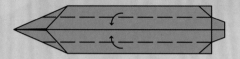

15. Make valley folds.

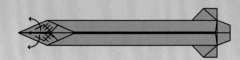

16. Make cuts and then valley folds.

17. Valley fold in half.

18. Valley fold top layers.

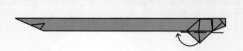

19. Valley fold bottom layers.

20. Rotate.

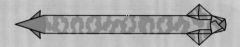

21. Add colors and patterns as desired.

22. Completed part 1.

Part 2

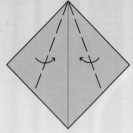

1. Kite fold.

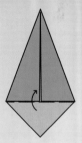

2. Valley fold.

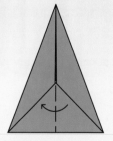

3. Valley fold in half.

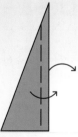

4. Valley fold top layer and mountain fold bottom layer.

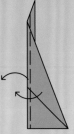

5. Valley fold top layer and mountain fold bottom layer.

6. Valley fold top layer.

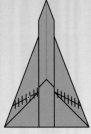

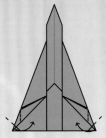

7. Make cuts as shown.

8. Make inside reverse folds.

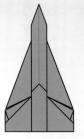

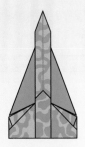

9. Add colors and patterns as desired.

10. Completed part 2.

TO ATTACH

 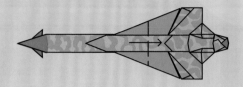

1. Insert part 2 into part 1 as indicated by the arrows.

2. Mountain fold and tuck in the bottom layer.

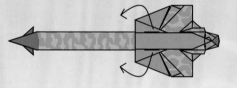 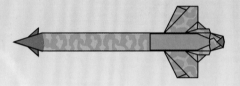

3. Make mountain folds.

4. Add additional colors and patterns as desired.

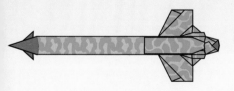

5. Completed Air-to-Surface Guided Missile.

Air-to-Air Anti-Aircraft Rocket

This air-to-air anti-aircraft rocket is loosely based on the R4M rocket, which was nicknamed Orkan (German for hurricane), a World War II era German rocket. It could also be used as an air-to-surface rocket with a maximum range of just under a mile (1,500 m), and a more accurate range of just under 2 feet (600 m). It weighs a compact 8.5 pounds (3.85 kg), has a length of approximately 32 inches (812 mm), and has a diameter of 2 inches (55 mm). The eight wing tips of the real R4M rocket stayed folded up until the anti-aircraft rocket was fired at the incoming missile or plane. Upon launching, it left behind a smoke trail responsible for the nickname of Hurricane.

Part 1

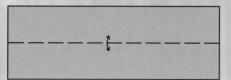

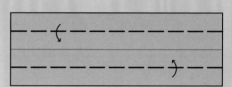

1. Start with a piece of the 3 $\frac{3}{4}$" x 9 $\frac{3}{4}$" paper. Valley fold in half and unfold.

2. Valley fold both sides to the center crease.

3. Make valley folds.

4. Make valley folds.

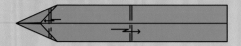

5. Make pleat folds.

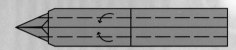

6. Make valley folds.

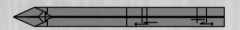

7. Make pleat folds.

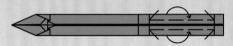

8. Make squash folds.

9. Make valley folds.

10. Completed part 1.

Part 2

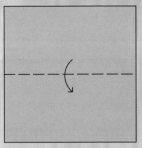

1. Start with an 8 1/2" by 8 1/2" paper. Valley fold in half.

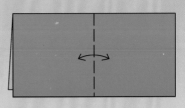

2. Valley fold and unfold.

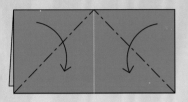

3. Make inside reverse folds.

4. Mountain fold.

5. Unfold the last fold.

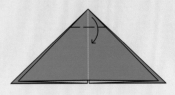

6. Valley fold.

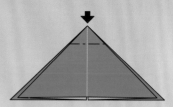

7. Unfold the last fold.

8. Sink fold by pushing inward along the creased lines.

9. Appearance before completion of sink fold.

10. Make cuts as shown.

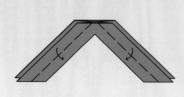

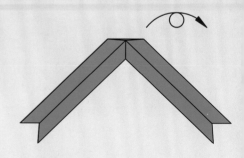

11. Make valley folds.

12. Turn over.

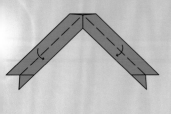

13. Make valley folds.

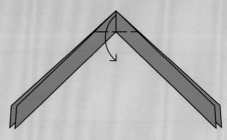

14. Valley fold and unfold.

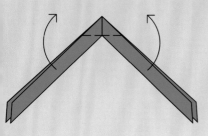

15. Make outside reverse folds.

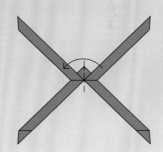

16. Valley fold.

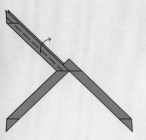

17. Valley fold.

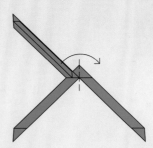

18. Valley fold.

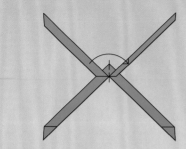

19. Valley fold.

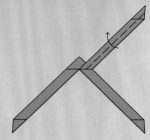

20. Valley fold.

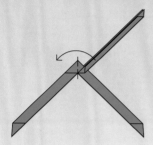

21. Valley fold.

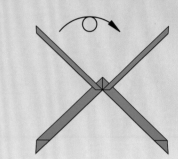

22. Turn over.

23. Valley fold and unfold.

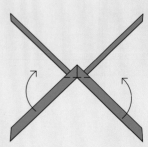

24. Make outside reverse folds.

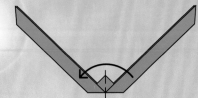

25. Valley fold.

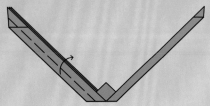

26. Valley fold.

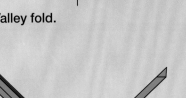

27. Valley fold.

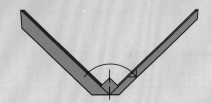

28. Valley fold.

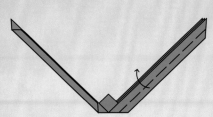

29. Valley fold.

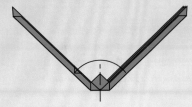

30. Valley fold.

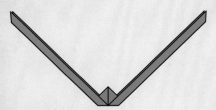

31. Separate all four legs.

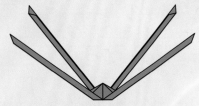

32. Completed part 2.

TO ATTACH

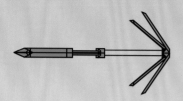

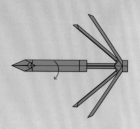

1. Insert part 1 into part 2 as shown and apply glue to hold.

2. Valley fold in half.

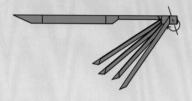

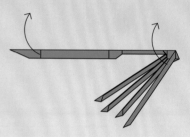

3. Inside reverse fold and tuck flap between layers. Apply glue to hold.

4. Make valley folds.

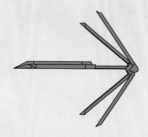

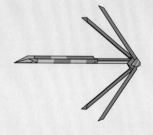

5. Add colors and patterns as desired.

6. Completed Air-to-Air Anti-Aircraft Rocket.

Manned Spacecraft

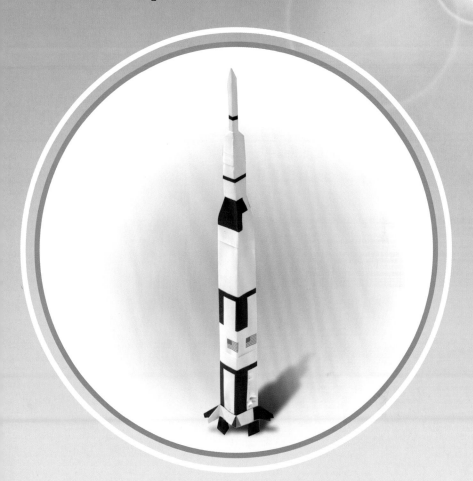

This manned space shuttle is based on NASA's famed Apollo 13 spacecraft. Launched on April 11, 1970, Apollo 13 was NASA's third manned spacecraft to go on a lunar-landing mission. The mission was not completed; an oxygen tank exploded on the third day of the mission—the mission then changed to one of survival. Despite limited power, water, heat, and oxygen, the crew safely landed on April 17, 1970, making the mission a "Successful Failure" according to NASA. The Apollo spacecraft has three parts: a command module, which housed the crew and flight controls; a service module, which housed the support system; and the lunar module, which the astronauts would take out on lunar landings. It was boosted into space by a rocket, which had a total length of 363 feet (110.6 m) and a diameter of 33 feet (10.1 m).

Part 1

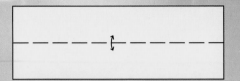

1. Start with a piece of the 3 3/4" x 9 3/4" paper. Valley fold in half and unfold.

2. Valley fold both sides to the center crease.

3. Valley fold both sides to the center crease and unfold.

4. Unfold folds from step 2.

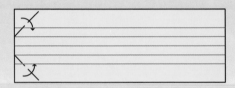

5. Make valley folds.

6. Make valley folds.

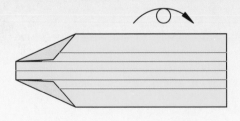

7. Turn over.

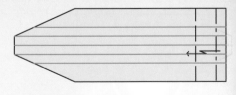

8. Pleat fold.

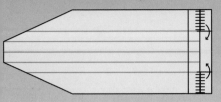

9. Make cuts and then valley folds.

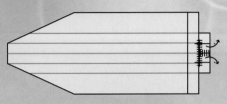

10. Make cuts and then mountain folds.

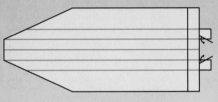

11. Make mountain folds.

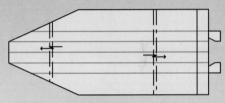

12. Make pleat folds.

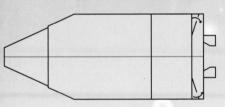

13. Make inside reverse folds.

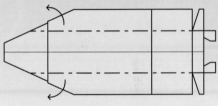

14. Make mountain folds and apply glue to hold in place.

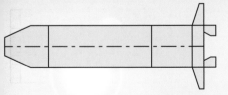

15. Mountain fold in half to crease slightly.

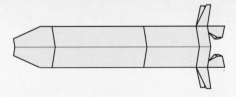

16. Completed part 1.

Part 2

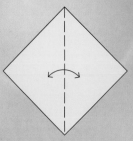

1. Start with a 4" by 4" paper. Valley fold and unfold.

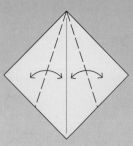

2. Kite fold and unfold.

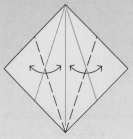

3. Make valley folds and unfold.

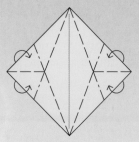

4. Pinch together at corners and fold inward.

5. Pleat fold.

6. Make valley folds.

7. Pleat fold.

8. Make valley folds.

9. Make cuts and then valley folds.

10. Valley fold.

11. Valley fold.

12. Make valley folds.

13. Valley fold.

14. Valley fold and apply glue to hold.

15. Valley fold.

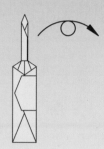

16. Turn over.

17. Mountain fold in half to crease slightly.

18. Completed part 2.

TO ATTACH

1. Insert part 2 into part 1 as shown and apply glue to hold.

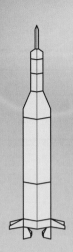

2. Add colors and patterns as desired.

3. Completed Manned Spacecraft.

Spaceship

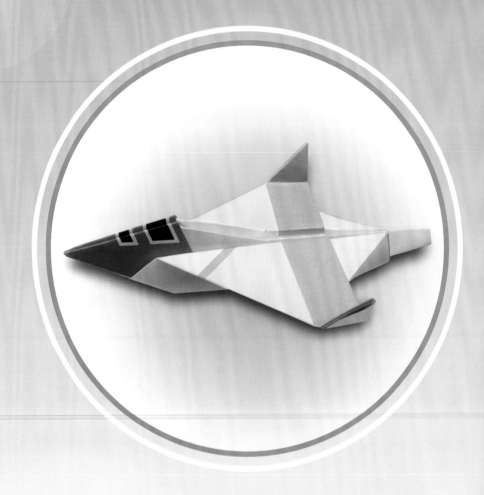

This science-fiction model is an imaginative figure that can soar through space at amazingly high speeds and can fight off any type of attack thrown its way.

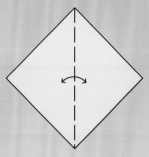

1. Valley fold and unfold.

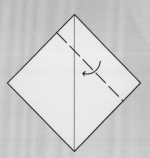

2. Valley fold.

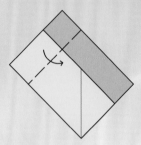

3. Valley fold.

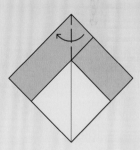

4. Valley fold.

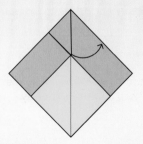

5. Pull and fold.

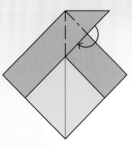

6. Squash fold.

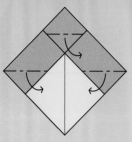

7. Make mountain folds.

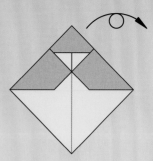

8. Turn over.

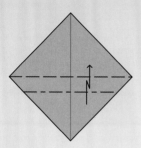

9. Pleat fold.

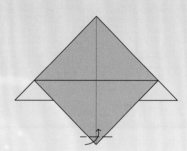

10. Valley fold.

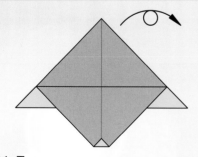

11. Turn over.

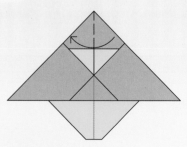

12. Valley fold.

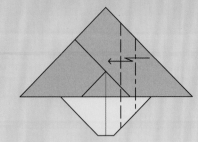 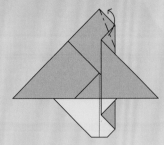

13. Pleat fold. **14. Mountain fold.**

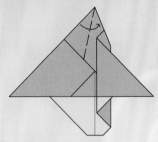 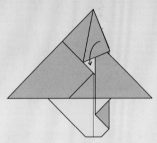

15. Valley fold top layer. **16. Hide top flap behind layers.**

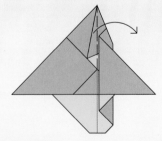 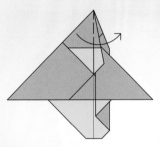

17. Valley fold. **18. Valley fold.**

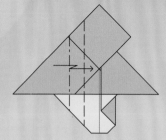

19. Pleat fold.

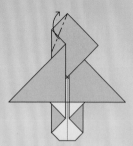

20. Mountain fold.

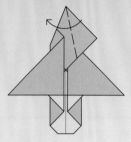

21. Valley fold.

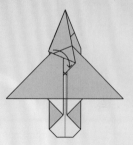

22. Hide top flap behind layers.

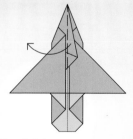

23. Valley fold.

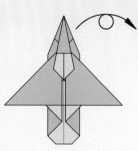

24. Turn over.

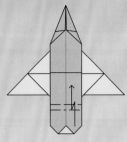

25. Pleat fold.

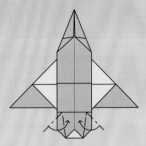

26. Make squash folds.

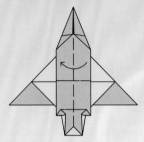

27. Valley fold in half.

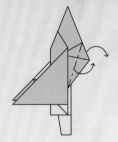

28. Make mountain folds.

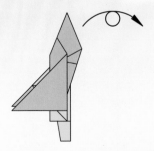

29. Rotate.

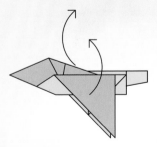

30. Make valley folds.

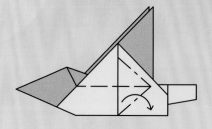

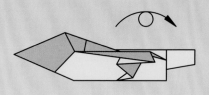

31. Make squash folds to level wings on both sides.

32. Rotate.

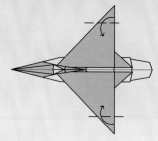

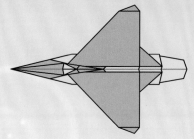

33. Make valley folds.

34. Add colors and patterns as desired.

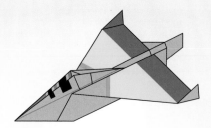

35. Completed Spaceship.

Flying Saucer

Another science-fiction model, this nifty imaginative figure can carry alien creatures to Earth at high speeds and without detection.

Part 1

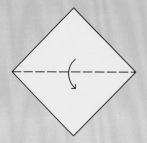

1. Valley fold in half.

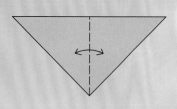

2. Valley fold and unfold.

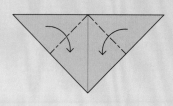

3. Make inside reverse folds.

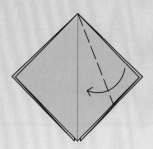

4. Valley fold.

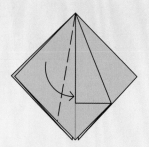

5. Valley fold.

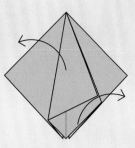

6. Unfold the last two folds.

7. Valley fold.

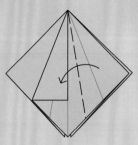

8. Valley fold.

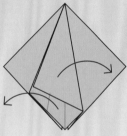

9. Unfold the last two folds.

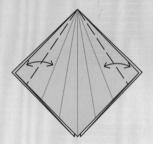

10. Make valley folds and then unfold.

11. Make inside reverse folds.

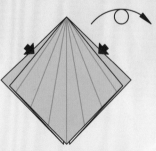

12. Apply glue to hold the last folds. Turn over.

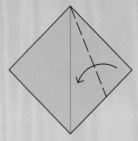

13. Valley fold top layer.

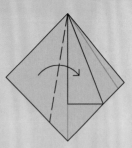

14. Valley fold top layer.

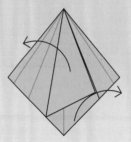

15. Unfold the last two folds.

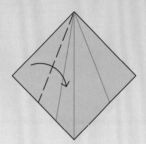

16. Valley fold top layer.

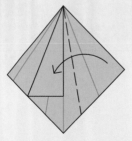

17. Valley fold top layer.

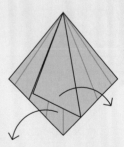

18. Unfold the last two folds.

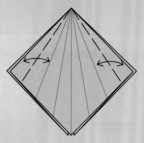

19. Make valley folds and then unfold.

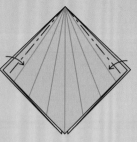

20. Make inside reverse folds.

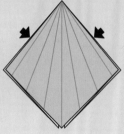

21. Apply glue to hold the last folds.

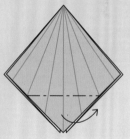

22. Mountain fold top layer.

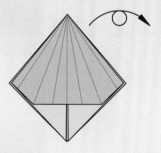

23. Turn over.

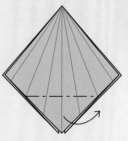

24. Mountain fold top layer.

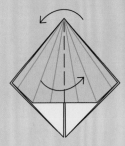

25. Valley fold to open flaps.

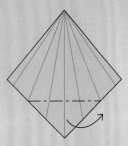

26. Mountain fold top layer.

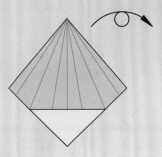

27. Turn over.

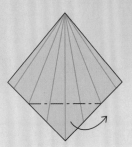

28. Mountain fold top layer.

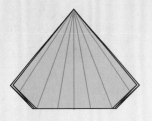

29. Flatten model.

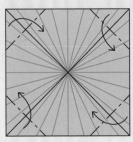

30. Make mountain folds.

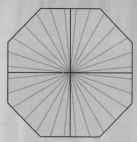

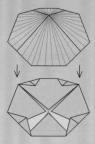

31. Completed mountain folds. Repeat steps 1–30 with another sheet of paper.

32. Place the two models together, folded sides facing in, and apply glue to hold.

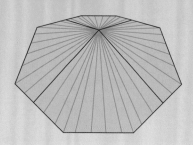

33. Completed part 1.

Part 2

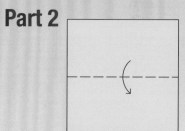

1. Valley fold in half.

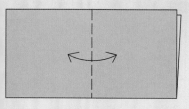

2. Valley fold and unfold.

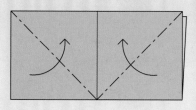

3. Make inside reverse folds.

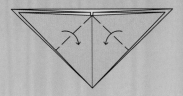

4. Make valley folds to the top layer.

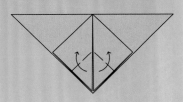

5. Make valley folds.

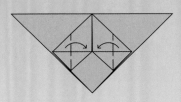

6. Make valley folds and apply glue to hold.

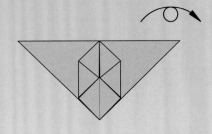

7. Turn over.

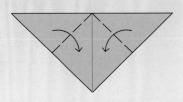

8. Make valley folds.

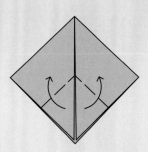

9. Make valley folds.

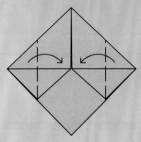

10. Make valley folds and apply glue to hold.

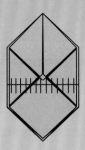

11. Make cut as shown.

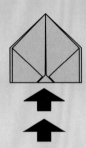

12. Insert your finger and push to inflate the paper.

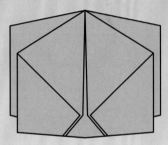

13. Completed part 2.

TO ATTACH

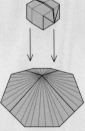

1. Join part 2 to part 1 as shown and apply glue to hold.

2. Completed Flying Saucer.

Space Shuttle

This model of a space shuttle is based on Russia's Buran spacecraft with a rocket engine. While it was built to be a reusable manned space shuttle, the Russians launched this model only once, in November 1988, unmanned. With a body length of 101 feet (30.78 m), a height of 53.64 feet (16.35 m), a diameter of 18 feet (5.49 m), and a wing span of 78.5 feet (23.92 m), this spacecraft had a landing speed of 1,056 miles per hour (1,700 km/hour).

Part 1

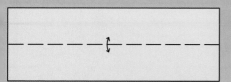

1. Start with a piece of the 3 3/4" x 9 3/4" paper. Valley fold in half and unfold.

2. Valley fold both sides to the center crease.

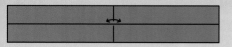

3. Valley fold and unfold.

4. Make valley folds.

5. Make valley folds, first to the four corners and then to the center.

6. Make inside reverse folds.

7. Turn over and add colors and
   patterns as desired.

8. Completed part 1.

Part 2

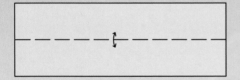

1. Start with a piece of the 3 3/4" x
   9 3/4" paper. Valley fold in half
   and unfold.

2. Valley fold both sides to the
   center crease.

3. Valley fold and unfold.

4. Make pleat folds.

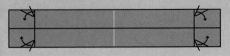

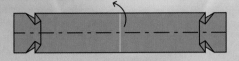

5. Make pleat folds.

6. Mountain fold in half.

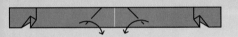

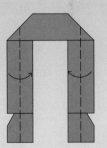

7. Make inside reverse folds.

8. Make valley folds to the top layers and mountain folds to the bottom layers.

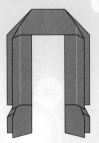

9. Add colors and patterns as desired.

10. Completed part 2.

Part 3

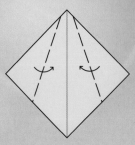

1. Start with a 4" by 4" paper.
   Make valley folds.

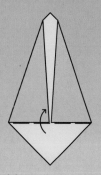

2. Valley fold.

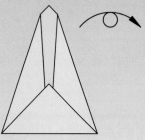

3. Turn over.

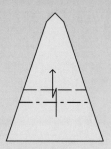

4. Pleat fold.

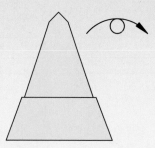

5. Turn over.

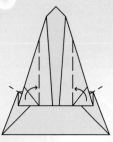

6. Make squash folds.

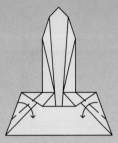

7. Make valley folds.

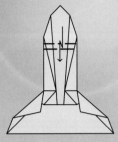

8. Pleat fold.

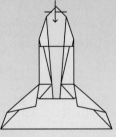

9. Valley fold.

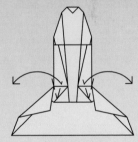

10. Make squash folds.

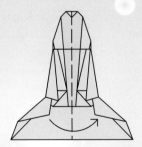

11. Valley fold in half.

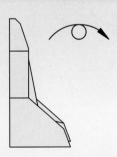

12. Rotate.

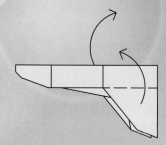

13. Valley fold top layer and
    mountain fold bottom layer.

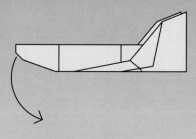

14. Pull and fold front tip.

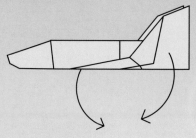

15. Fold the wings to balance.

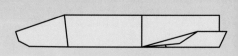

16. Add colors and patterns as
    desired.

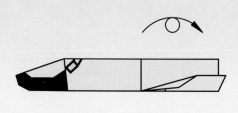

17. Rotate.

18. Completed part 3.

Part 4

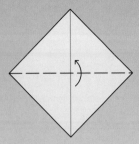

1. Start with a 3" by 3" paper. Valley fold.

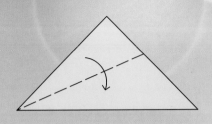

2. Valley fold top layer.

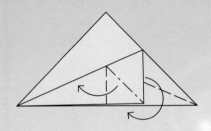

3. Squash fold.

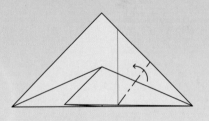

4. Inside reverse fold.

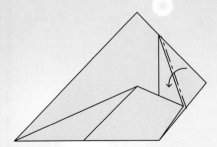

5. Inside reverse fold.

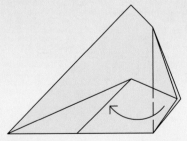

6. Valley fold.

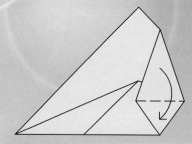

7. Valley fold.

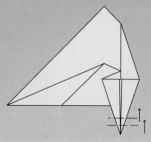

8. Make valley folds.

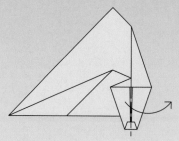

9. Valley fold.

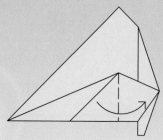

10. Valley fold.

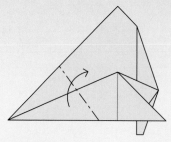

11. Inside reverse fold.

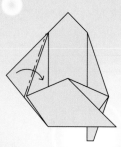

12. Inside reverse fold.

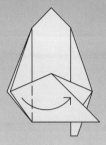

13. Valley fold.

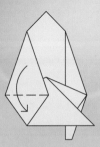

14. Valley fold.

15. Make valley folds.

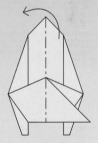

16. Mountain fold top layer.

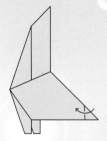

17. Inside reverse fold.

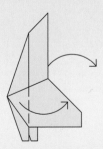

18. Valley fold top layer and mountain fold bottom layer.

19. Add colors and pattern as desired.

20. Completed part 4.

TO ATTACH

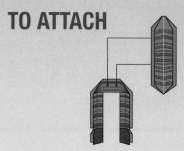

1. Insert part 2 between the center layers of part 1 and apply glue to hold.

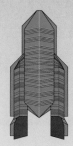

2. Completed first assembly.

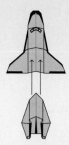

3. Insert part 4 over part 3 as shown.

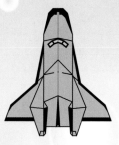

4. Mountain fold to tuck in the back layer.

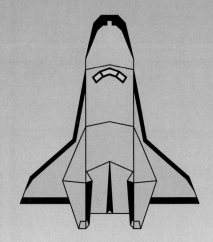

5. Completed second assembly.

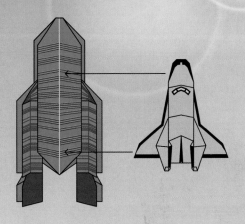

6. Join second assembly to first
   assembly and apply glue to hold.

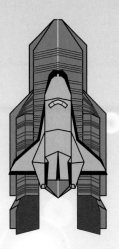

7. Completed Space Shuttle.

Index